To Janet and Mark

Christmas 1978

These stories are the Aboriginal explanations
of how some things came to being, particularly
animals and places in the far north of
Australia. We hope you enjoy reading and
learning about the culture of the true Australians

Love Maggie and Rick.

People of the Dreamtime

PEOPLE OF THE DREAMTIME

ALAN MARSHALL

Illustrated by Miriam-Rose Ungunmerr

Hyland House Melbourne

First published 1952
Second edition with new illustrations published in 1978 by
HYLAND HOUSE PUBLISHING PTY LIMITED
10 Hyland Street
South Yarra
Melbourne
Victoria 3141

Published with the support of the Aboriginal Arts Board of
the Australia Council

Text © Alan Marshall 1978
Illustrations © Miriam-Rose Ungunmerr 1978

Marshall, Alan, 1902–
    People of the dreamtime.
    ISBN 0 908090 03 x
    1. Aborigines, Australian—Legends.   I. Title.
398.2'0994

Typeset by Asco Trade Typesetting Limited, Hong Kong
Printed by Toppan Printing Company (H.K.) Ltd

FOREWORD

At the time when that humane and gentle man, Alan Marshall, was collecting these stories and adapting them for publication, white Australians were just emerging from the trauma of a war which had threatened to take this country out of the possession of the European race. We had then discovered in ourselves a love for the physical and perceptible aspects of the island continent, which took us almost by surprise. For in the brief history of our occupation, there had been little love or respect, and much harsh exploitation and opposition; while for its first human inhabitants we had little sympathy or even interest. The Aborigines, for whom this country was a basic spiritual as well as material resource, had become outcasts, landless in their own places; many tribes had not even been allowed the privilege of survival.

In the upsurge of further exploitation that followed World War II, when even the most remote parts of the country were thrown open to the demands of Western technology and consumption that dawning sense of a bond with the land itself was again smothered. It was not for decades that the sheer impact of our assault began to rouse concern, and not for decades that we began to feel some sense of responsibility for the plight of Aborigines whose last remaining places were being invaded.

But at least the Aborigines were making their voices heard in the work of their own writers and spokesmen, and through anthropologists like A.P. Elkin and others. The anthropologists taught that there was much to respect in those lives and ways of living which were so different from ours, while the Aborigines told us something of what they were suffering.

The remnants of legend salvaged by a few recorders such as Mrs Langloh Parker from the largely vanished tribes, and by Alan Marshall himself, can tell us very little of the reality of which they were part, which through dance, song, story, art and decoration expressed the totality of Aboriginal life in relation to this country. That web of religion and knowledge, that whole way of seeing, have been torn apart and scattered as though they were no more than worthless fantasy. The work of men like Professor W.E.H. Stanner, whose interpretations of surviving myth in places still largely untouched go so deep, cannot be applied to what is already lost.

We ourselves had come here already dispossessed, not only of the countries we came from, but of our own inner unity. Laurens van der Post, interpreter of the African Bushmen, has spoken of 'the peril of man when divorced from the first things in himself', the peril of the loss of meaning in life. 'Cut off by accumulated knowledge from the heart of his own living experience, he moves among a comfortable rubble of material possessions, alone and unbelonging, sick, poor, starved of meaning.' (*The Heart of the Hunter*) It seems to me that this is a most accurate description of the lives of white Australians in a country to which they know they have no abiding title nor depth of relationship.

The stories in this book come from a way of living which will always be alien to us. We will never be able to feel in ourselves any relationship of kinship with mountains, stars, moon and sun, trees and animals. Even Marshall himself may sometimes have edited, misinterpreted or misunderstood the words he heard, for like us all he is an inheritor of attitudes which keep us alien from the earth. The times before time, when aspects of ourselves were merged—not imaged—in the natural world, are inaccessible to our disinherited age. But it would be quite wrong to think that these stories are no more than moral tales or childish fancies. Like dreams, they have meanings we have forgotten or never known.

For all that, we can understand and respond to much in them. Any woman can feel why it was Kurramon, the brother who was thin and weak but who received strength from his mother's grave before he wooed her, who won the soul-woman Lamari against the material gifts his greedier brothers made, in the story of the 'Rainbow and the bread-fruit flower'. Any man with a knowledge of his own motives will see why the Whale, who valued friendship only when it was to his advantage, had to lose his precious canoe. If many of the elements in the stories are lost to us, we can share the truths they tell.

This re-issue is illuminated by Miriam-Rose Ungunmerr's remarkable paintings. As a member of the Moil tribe near the Daly River, she is in touch with the life of her people; as one of those Aborigines who are beginning to offer us tentatively a strand to bridge the gulf between white and black ways of seeing, she has gifts for us too. Unless we can somehow strengthen that small bridge, we whites will never begin to heal the wounds we have inflicted on ourselves as well as on the people we have wronged. These illustrations speak for themselves and need no words from me.

JUDITH WRIGHT
May 1978

CONTENTS

INTRODUCTION

I spent nine months in Arnhem Land during 1945–6 and it was here I heard these Dreamtime stories.

In those days there was no mining in Arnhem Land and large tracts of bushland were trackless and unexplored. Each tribal group spoke a different language: people from Oenpelli could not understand the language of those who came from Milingimbi, and the 'wild' natives of Caledon Bay and the Liverpool River areas were 'foreigners' to the natives of the Aborigines Mission at Roper River.

But although communication under such circumstances was difficult, it was not impossible. I was fortunate in having the services of one or two Blacks who understood English or enough words of this language to make their stories vivid and alive.

One such man was called Marawana and he lived at Oenpelli. Here are my comments on Marawana taken from my book *These were my Tribesmen*.

'The animals of Marawana's stories did not express themselves in the stylized sentences one imagined would be characteristic of traditional legends. Their personalities emerged uncoloured by any attempt to present them as cult-heroes existing in a world untouched by human frailty.

'Their conversation was strikingly human and recreated them so vividly that they stepped from their past world of shadows and became the living companions of today.

'The legends of Western peoples feature men of majesty and power or heroes notable for deeds of prowess and courage, but the men and women who, in the guise of animals, move through the lovely stories of the Blacks, are counterparts of the average human being.

'The dog in Marawana's story, "The dog and the kangaroo", was such a person. I liked him. He seemed so natural and never for a moment spoke in the manner of one whose every remark was destined to be repeated by a multitude of people before it finally reached the pages of my note book. He was not interested in posterity; he was only interested in his friend, the kangaroo. This story is supposed to explain the origin of painting and suggests the reason why, in every native drawing of a kangaroo, the animal is pictured in death, lying prostrate on the ground.'

Makarrwola, a Milingimbi man of high degree, told me the story of the moon's origin, a tale he unfolded while squatting in the darkness of a mia-mia. A thunderstorm was raging outside as his voice continued its chanting and merged with and became part of the sound of the wind as it forced the trees to bow before its power. The lightning sometimes illuminated the faces of other natives who had crept in to hear the stories. A little girl stood behind me for the entire evening. She had rested her hand on the top of my head and there it remained, its weight no greater than a leaf.

There is one story included in these myths, 'The Girl who made dilly bags', that I never collected from the Blacks. It was told to me by Nettie Palmer, the wife of Vance Palmer the Australian novelist, when both these people were alive. She said it appeared, in an abbreviated form, in a diary written by a Queensland cattleman. She suggested I enlarge it to a story that would increase the size of my book to the length demanded by the publisher. In the first edition I failed to acknowledge the source of this story, so I do so now with gratitude to the man who collected its outline from the Blacks. From the information given to me by Nettie Palmer, I shaped the story as it appears here. I have forgotten the name of the man Nettie Palmer quoted, but I am sure you will notice the difference in style between his tale and the other stories.

I am glad this collection has again been published. It is twenty-six years since it first appeared and those Blacks who still remain rarely get an opportunity to hear the stories of their people: the Songmen sing no more.

My publisher was fortunate to secure the services of Miriam-Rose Ungunmerr to illustrate the stories. She painted illustrations for all the stories except one, 'The Origin of the Bull-roarer'. For tribal reasons Mrs Ungunmerr was not allowed to illustrate this story which features a sacred object that the women of her tribe are not allowed to see. Mrs Ungunmerr is a full blood Aborigine from the Moil Tribe between Port Keats and Daly River. She was one of the first full blood Aborigines to be employed by the Commonwealth teaching service. She is also the author of a book called *The Nature of Aboriginal Children*.

To my friend
VIC LESLIE

Who led me to the
Blacks of Arnhem Land

The dog
and the kangaroo

When the kangaroo and the dog were men
they met on a track in the bush.

'Where are you going, Dog?'
asked the kangaroo.
'I am going hunting,'
replied the dog.
'I'd like to go with you,'
said the kangaroo.
'All right,' said the dog.
'You can come with me and be my friend.'

After they had gathered their spears and
their woomeras the kangaroo asked,
'Where will we go?'
'We will go this way,'
said the dog
and he led the kangaroo towards the hills.

After they had gone a little way
they came to a creek.
The banks of the creek were of clay.
There was brown clay and red clay and white clay.
They dug into the bank with their spears
and soon they had heaps of coloured clays beside them.

'You try and write me,' the dog said to the kangaroo.
'Draw me like a dog.'
'All right,' said the kangaroo. 'I'll draw you like a dog.'
'Write me in brown clay first,' the dog said.
'Try and turn me into a dog.'
The kangaroo drew his head first, then his neck
and belly and chest and tail and four legs.

'Eh, wah!' he said.
'I've got you down. I write you properly.
You are just like a dog.'
'That's good,' said the dog.
'You've made me like a dog.'

'Now you write me like I did you,' said the kangaroo.
'All right,' said the dog. 'You lie down.'
'Don't write me baddest way,' said the kangaroo.
'You just lie down,' said the dog.
'I'll write you just like a kangaroo
so that you'll go hop, hop, hop all the way.'

The dog drew the kangaroo's head,
then his two arms,
then his belly and tail and two back legs.

'There you are,'
he said when he had finished.
'I've got you right.
I've put everything into your body.'
'If you've put everything into me
I must be just like a kangaroo,'
said the kangaroo.
'Everything you have is there,'
said the dog.

'Now, you try and bark like a dog,'
said the kangaroo.
'All right,' said the dog and he barked like a dog.

'Now chase me,' said the kangaroo.
'We will only go a little way.'
'You take the lead to me,' said the dog.
'I'll run behind you.'

Now they were men no longer;
they were a dog and a kangaroo.

14

The kangaroo bounded away
and the dog followed behind him.
They went across a valley and over a creek
and up the side of a hill,
the dog barking all the way.
Then they stopped to rest.

'What will we call that place
where we write ourselves?'
asked the dog.
'I don't know what we will call that place,'
said the kangaroo.
'We will call it Barl-barl,' said the dog.

'Let us run again,' said the kangaroo.
'All right,' said the dog.
'You take the lead to me again.
I'll bark behind you.'
They ran for a long way.
They crossed another creek and
came to a place where there was a huge rock
at the foot of a mountain.

'This is a good place,' said the dog.
'We will climb to the top of that rock.'
'All right,' said the kangaroo.
'You bite my tail so that I will jump
on to the top of that rock.'

When the dog had climbed up beside him, the dog said,
'What will we call this place?'
'We will call this place
Numilukari and Beenameenami,'
said the kangaroo.
'All right,' said the dog.
'Now we live here.'
And they lived there,
and the dog barked all day.

15

The little girl
and the snake

In the long ago
a woman and a little girl
lived at Cooper's Creek.
The woman was the mother of the little girl
and she had promised her to a man in marriage.

The little girl was frightened of the man,
and the man knew this.
He had sharp, black eyes,
and when he looked at her
his eyes were very still.

One day the man got some grass
and put it inside a hollow log.
Then he crept inside the log and
turned into a snake.

A brown bird alighted near the log
and the snake called out to it,
'You come and see me
and you come and talk to me
while I am inside the hollow log.'
'All right,'
said the brown bird.

The mother heard the brown bird
talk to that snake
and she called out,
'Hey, brown bird,
what is in that hollow log over there?'

But the brown bird became frightened
and flew away.

The little girl walked over to the hollow log
and looked inside it.
It was dark in there and for a moment
she could not see anything.
Then she saw two still eyes glowing from the dark.
She sang out to her mother,
'Mother, come and see.'
The mother came over and looked up that log,
but no eyes glowed at her.
'There's nothing there,'
the mother said.
The little girl looked again
and saw the eyes.
'There's something there, mother.'
'Well, I can't see it,'
said the mother.
'I can see it,'
said the little girl.
'It is two eyes.'
'If there is something there,'
said the mother,
'we will hunt it out.
Get me a long stick.'

When the little girl had got the long stick
the mother said,
'I will go to the other end
and poke down the log with the long stick.
You put your hand inside the log at this end
and grab what is there.'
The little girl thrust her hand into the hollow log
and when her mother poked
the long stick up the other end
the snake bit the little girl.
The little girl sprang back
and the snake crawled out and said,
'Black, red and yellow, now they call me snake.
I can bite everybody in the world.'

Then he turned and crawled away,
and all that day he crawled
until he reached his own country.
Here he found a large rock
and at the foot of this rock he rested.
'I must camp here by this rock,'
he said.
'I was a man once,
now I am a snake.
I will call myself
Yerabartbart.'

He picked up a hollow stick
and threw it into the lagoon.
After he had done this
he crawled into a big hole in the rock
and called the hole
Babartjayo,
and he is there today.

The Milky Way

In the days when Priepriggie lived,
the sky was trackless.
The stars were young and vigorous and they lived alone,
for there was no road whereby they might traverse the sky
and dance one with the other
when the nights were long.
These were the days before the Milky Way.

On earth, the people were happy
and danced and sang before camp fires laden with game.
The tracks from here to there were many
and were trodden smooth by the feet of friends.

Priepriggie lived at Ward Point
at the mouth of the Pine River in the Cape Country.
He was a Songman and a dancer.
When the bull-roarers thrummed from the darkness
and the ceremonial clay was painted thick
upon his tribal brothers,
he led the dancing and the chanting.
And the songs they sung
were the songs of Priepriggie
and the steps they danced were those he had created.
So he was loved by the people
and grew strong and upright,
happy in the strength of their regard.

On a morning when the flying foxes had returned
from their feeding grounds
and the noise of their bickering had ceased,
Priepriggie rose and took his spear and woomera
and went down to the mangroves
to spear some for food.

That night there was to be feasting.
The tribes had gathered for a corroboree.
The men would beat their throwing sticks,
slap their thighs and pound their feet
to the dances of Priepriggie.
His songs would stir them,
his steps would give them grace.

But food was needed for the feasting
and Priepriggie was also a hunter.
The sun had not yet coloured the Eastern sky,
but the piccaninny dawn revealed the dark bats
hanging like fruit
from the mangrove trees.
Priepriggie moved stealthily
through the covered darkness then
stopped beneath a huge tree heavy with their weight.
The biggest and strongest of all
flying foxes slept there.
A great strength and power enveloped this tree.

Priepriggie hooked his woomera to the end of his spear
then threw back his shoulder for the cast.
He hurled his spear
and as it sped upwards there came a great flash
and the roar of a thousand furious wings.
The mangroves thrashed their limbs in a mighty wind,
but above the wind could be heard shouts and cries
as from a multitude in rage.
The flying foxes swooped from the tree-tops
and hurtled through the dark corridors
between the mangrove trunks like spirits in fear.
And they came down upon Priepriggie
and seized him and bore him aloft.
They burst through the canopy of leaves
into a dawn of flaming sky,
and the wings of those that carried him
were black against the red.

And Priepriggie's people heard the wings go by
and they ran from their mia-mias
and from their resting places beneath trees
and they saw him pass.
The visiting tribesmen, roused from sleep,
saw him shooting skywards like a star.
Behind him trailed a pathway of smoke
such was the speed of his travel.

When the wings were silent and the smoke had gone,
those who watched
heard the voice of Priepriggie
coming from some sky-place beyond the last star.
He sang them his last song.
It was the last song of Priepriggie
and it came from the sky
where he would sing no more.
And in the song he bade them goodbye.

As they listened a new dance was born in them
and they moved their legs and arms and tossed their heads
and sang the last song of Priepriggie
as he sang it to them.
That night they sang it.
Priepriggie's people
and the people of other tribes
gathered for the corroboree,
they all sang it.
And they danced the dance of Priepriggie's last song.
Of all dances it was the best
and of all songs Priepriggie's last song was the greatest.
They looked up as they sang and danced,
and there across the sky
stretched the Milky Way.
And it had never been there before.

The Jabiru and the Crow

In the days when the Jabiru and the Crow were men
the Jabiru sent a message to the Crow.
'I have caught a lot of fish in my fish net,' he said.
'Come and eat some fish with me.'
And the Crow said, 'Right.'

Then the Crow got his dilly bag and his stone axe
and he set off to visit the Jabiru.
It was cold and he was hungry
and he thought of the fish the Jabiru had caught.
'The Jabiru is a good fellow,'
he said to himself.
'It is a fine thing to have a friend like the Jabiru.'

As he walked along the track
he saw some bees flying into a hole
in the trunk of a tree.
'Ah, sugar bag!' he exclaimed.
'Now I will be able to eat sugar bag before I eat fish.'
He climbed the tree
and with his stone axe
cut a hole in the trunk where the bees were entering.
He thrust his hand into the hole
and drew forth some comb dripping with honey.
When he had eaten it he took some more
and he ate and ate till all the honey had gone.
He did not keep any to give the Jabiru.
'Jabiru has plenty fish,'
he said as he washed his hands in the creek.
'I have no fish.'

When he drew near to the Jabiru's camp
he saw the Jabiru cooking fish over his camp fire.

The Jabiru saw him and called out,
'Come and sit over here. I have a lot of fish for you.'
As soon as the Crow sat down
he took a big mullet and began to eat it.
'That is a very good fish you are eating,'
said the Jabiru.
'As soon as you finish it let us sit down and talk together.'

While the Crow was eating the Jabiru sat and watched him.
Suddenly he saw a bee and some sugar bag
in the Crow's hair.
'Hullo!' he exclaimed.
'I see a bee and some sugar bag in your hair.'
The Crow didn't reply. He kept on eating.

The Jabiru sat thinking.
Then he said, 'Don't you eat any more fish now
or you will spoil my fishing
and I will never get any more.
When I throw my net in the creek
I won't be able to catch them.
When the fish see that bee and that sugar bag
in your hair
it will frighten them away.'
When the Crow heard this
he rose to his feet and walked away.
He sat on a log and did not speak to the Jabiru.

The Jabiru sat there and thought about the Crow.
'Why did you walk over there?' he called out at last.
'Because I might eat your fish,' said the Crow.
'If I eat your fish the fish will see
the bee and the sugar bag in my hair
and then you will never be able to catch
any more fish with your fishing net.'
'You don't want to talk like that,' said the Jabiru.
'This is your country. You can do what you like.
Come and eat some more fish.'

26

'No,' the Crow said.
'I can't eat your fish,
I would spoil your fishing.
When you throw your net into the creek
you won't catch any fish.
I'm sorry, Jabiru, but I can't eat any more of your fish.'

But the Jabiru thought he could make the Crow
change his mind and he kept repeating,
'Come and eat some more fish,'
and the Crow kept answering him,
'No, I can't. If I do,
you won't catch any fish
when you throw your net into the creek in the morning.'
Finally the Crow got angry
and he rose and said, 'Goodbye.
I am going home to my country where I come from,'
and he walked away without looking back at the Jabiru.

The Crow lived on the side of a rocky mountain
and the name of the mountain was Arguloop.
Here he lived in a cave
and below the cave was a wide swamp
where the magpie geese nested.
Soon the geese began laying their eggs
and the Crow took his dilly bag
and went down to the swamp to gather some for food.
There were so many eggs
that he soon filled his dilly bag.
So he carried it up to his cave and returned for more.
When he had a big pile of goose eggs in his cave
he sent a message to the Jabiru:
'Come and eat goose eggs with me.
I have a lot of goose eggs.'
When the Jabiru received the message he said,
'All right, I'll go.
I'd like to see the Crow,
see how he is getting on.'

27

So he set off to visit the Crow
and when he reached the cave the Crow greeted him:
'Hullo, my friend.
I've got a lot of goose eggs for you.'
The Crow built a big fire and roasted the eggs,
then he said to the Jabiru,
'Come and sit down over here and I'll give you some eggs.
This is a better place here.'
The Jabiru sat down and took an egg and began eating it.

While he was eating,
the Crow looked steadily at him
and he saw some green ants in the Jabiru's hair.
'Hullo!' he exclaimed.
'You've been eating green ants.
If you've been eating green ants
you'll spoil the goose eggs.
All the goose eggs go away
when you eat the green ants.
If a man eats goose eggs he can never eat green ants,
and if he eats green ants he can never eat goose eggs.
You are the first man I've ever seen
to eat goose eggs after green ants.
That is all I have to say to you, Jabiru.'
'All right,' said the Jabiru.
'I say goodbye to you.'
'And I say goodbye to you, too,' said the Crow.
'I hope I never see you again.'
'And I hope I never see you again,' said the Jabiru.
'I will never send any more messages to you,'
and he walked away.

This is why
the Jabiru and the Crow are never seen together.

The origin
of Mount Nimbuwah

In the beginning,
Nimbuwah was a rainbow,
but he grew tired of his lonely life
and he came down to earth
and turned into a barramunda fish.

From his home in the sky
he had often seen
a woman diving for water-lily roots
in a lagoon
while her two children played on the bank.
She was beautiful
and when she emerged wet from the water of the lagoon
she gleamed like a brown fish.

Nimbuwah fell in love with her,
and when he became a barramunda fish
he made his home in the lagoon of water-lilies
so that he could be near her.

One day the mother and her two children
were standing on the bank of the lagoon
and the mother heard two fish-hawks talking.
'See, there is a fish,' said one.
'It is a very big fish
and would be too heavy for us to lift.'
'Did you hear that fish-hawk?'
the mother asked her little girl.
'There must be a big fish here.'
She got a long stick with a sharp point,
then she said to the little boy,
'You stand here with your sister.
Don't go near the water.'

29

The mother stood on the edge of the water
and looked for the fish.
Then she saw it just below the surface,
and the water in which it was resting was shallow,
so she stepped into the water
and thrust at the fish with her stick.
But the fish moved and she missed it.
She tried again,
and again she missed it.
While she was doing this the water was slowly rising,
and the fish was getting bigger and bigger.

The little girl, watching her, grew afraid
and she called out,
'Mother, you must kill it.
It must be something, mother.'
'It is a big fish,' replied the mother.
'I will catch it,'
and again she struck at the fish,
but again she missed it.
And the water was getting deeper and deeper
and the fish bigger and bigger.
And the mother kept striking with her stick,
and the water kept rising,
and the fish kept growing.

Suddenly the fish swam beneath the woman
and it lifted her on its back and carried her away.
It carried her to its own country
and there it turned into a stone mountain
and the woman into a column of stone beside it.

The little girl and the little boy ran home to their father
and the little girl said,
'Father, we have something terrible to tell you
about our mother.
Our mother saw a fish,
but it wasn't a fish and it took her away.'

The father took his stone axe and he said,
'I will go and cut his head off. It is Nimbuwah.'

And he walked till he came to the mountain
and he cut at its rocky head with his axe,
and when he had nearly cut its head off
he turned to stone
and there he stands today
beside the stone of his wife
and the stone of Nimbuwah.

That is how Mount Nimbuwah in Arnhem Land
has a crown like a head with a half-severed neck,
and that is why,
standing beside it,
are two columns of stone.

Loolo, the blue fish, and Nullandi, the moon

In the Dreamtime
before the moon was born
there lived two men.
One was called Loolo and the other Nullandi.
They were married men and both had children.

Nullandi was a happy man
who played with his children
when he returned from the hunt.
He made rush spears for his sons
and carved wooden toys for his daughters.
His wife's dilly bag was never empty,
for she knew where to find the biggest yams
and the longest water-lily roots in their country.
'My wife is a good woman,' he would say.

Loolo was a sad man
and scowled at his children when they spoke to him.
He was for ever complaining
of the scarcity of food,
yet found no pleasure in the spearing of a kangaroo.
'This will be our last meat for many days,'
he would say.
'There are fewer kangaroos than there were.'

He was afraid of death
and of old age
and of sickness
and grew moody and depressed
when these subjects were mentioned.
He often argued with Nullandi
whose smiling face offended him
and whose happiness he could not understand.

33

One day,
when they were returning unladen
from the chase,
Loolo grew bitter at Nullandi's cheerfulness,
for he knew
that Nullandi was thinking of his children
and of how he would play with them
when they reached the camp.
Loolo couldn't play with his children
for they were afraid of him.

'We are like kangaroos,'
he said to Nullandi.
'Kangaroos get killed
and that is the end of them.
I am going to die some day.
I know I will never live for ever.
I will leave my wife and children
and I will never see them again.
I will be dead.
There is no life after death.
There is only death.'

'I am not going to die,'
said Nullandi.
'No, never.
I will have a short death
then I will live again.
My wife and my children will be always mine.
They will live again as I live again.'

'I will never see my wife and children again
when I am dead,' said Loolo.
I will be dead for ever.'

Nullandi replied,
'I am going to die over there,'
and he pointed to the East.

34

'I will be the moon,
and have a short death
then come alive again.
You say you are going to die forever,
then you will die forever.
You will leave your bones
and your bones will never know you again.
You will become a blue fish when you die,
a blue fish in the sea.'

'You and all people will die forever,'
said Loolo.
'Everyone will be like me—
die and be dead
and never live again.'

'No,' said Nullandi.
'People will be like me when I am the moon.
They will have a short death then live again.'
Then they parted and their friendship was finished.

When they were old
and it came their time to die,
Nullandi turned into the moon
as he had said
and he died only to live again.
And Loolo became the blue fish
and he died forever
as he had said
and his bones lay on the beach.

The Winjarning brothers

In the days before the ants
there lived a tribe of strange people.
When these people raised their arms
great wings grew upon them
and with these wings they could fly
like bats.
They were called the Keeng Keeng
and they were feared by all the tribes.

The Keeng Keeng were cruel
and deceitful
and they lived in a large cave in the mountains.
In the centre of this cave
was a huge pit of fire
and in this pit dwelt a Fire God
who was worshipped by the Keeng Keeng.
The Keeng Keeng
sacrificed human beings to this god;
they cast bound men into the pit of fire
and there the god devoured them.

One day,
two men of the Keeng Keeng
were flying over the hills and valleys
looking for a human being they could sacrifice.
Far beneath them
they saw the Winjarning brothers
returning from the hunt.
These brothers were men of high degree
and were known throughout the tribes
for their skill in healing the sick.
They were always willing to help those in distress
and because of this they were loved.

The two Keeng Keeng alighted near the brothers
and walked over to them.
The brothers greeted them in friendly fashion
as was their habit.
They knew the Keeng Keeng were dangerous
and sacrificed human beings to their Fire God
but when the Keeng Keeng invited them to their cave
to be welcomed by their tribe
they agreed to accompany them,
for they had faith in themselves
and in their strength.
They were also curious
to see these people in their own surroundings.

When they arrived at the cave
the Winjarning brothers were made welcome
and asked to stay for a few days
so that they could enjoy the feasting
and the dancing
that the Keeng Keeng would provide
for their pleasure.

So the brothers stayed
for three days,
and on the third day
they announced
that they were leaving for their own country.
When the Keeng Keeng heard this
they pleaded with the brothers
to stay one more day
so that they could see
the sacred emu dance
of the women.
The Winjarning brothers knew
that the sacred emu dance
always preceded the sacrifice,
but they stayed,
for their curiosity was greater than their fear.

The sacred emu dance took place beside the fire pit,
so that the flames from the pit
cast the shadows of the dancers
upon the wall.
Only the young girls of the Keeng Keeng danced.
They formed a circle
and moved in and out like emus feeding.
Each held an arm aloft
and the shadows of the arms
were the necks of the emus
that bowed and strutted upon the wall.
The shadow-emus moved with the girls
and sometimes they were large
and menacing
and sometimes they shrunk to the size of a maid.

The Winjarning brothers
would have forgotten all else
save the shadows,
for the shadows in their play
held the eyes like a spell.
But their minds were keen
and their danger was always with them.

The Keeng Keeng watched the brothers,
and when the brothers seemed to have forgotten
all else save the shadows,
they rose stealthily to their feet
and moved in upon them.
But the elder of the Winjarning brothers
saw them moving beyond the firelight.
He saw their teeth,
white in the dark,
and their eyes
like fire without flame.
He leapt to his feet as they rushed,
and their arms grasped
the place that he had left.

So swift was his leap
that he failed to grasp the spears beside him,
thus he had no weapon
with which to defend himself.
He ran round the rim of the fire pit,
the Keeng Keeng screaming behind him.
Round and round the fire pit he ran,
and the Keeng Keeng,
less swift than he,
moved closer to the pit's rim
so that the distance they traversed would be lessened.
But they grew dizzy as they ran,
and one by one
they fell into the fire pit
where the Fire God awaited them.
As they fell,
the flames leaped high in wrath
and they were devoured in a great heat.
Then the last Keeng Keeng screamed and fell
and there were no more Keeng Keeng men in the world.

The Winjarning brothers ran from the cave
and went far into the bush,
but next day they returned
to see if the fire pit was still aflame.
The cave had gone,
and where the pit of fire had burned
there was an ant-hill
and hundreds of ants were running
in and out of the hill,
and some of the ants had wings.

Thereafter ants lived in the world.

The Whowie

Only a few animals remain now
and those that remain are small.
Once there were many animals
and some of them were as high as a tree.
Most of the big animals ate grass,
but the Whowie ate men.

The Whowie
was longer than a tree that lies on the ground
and when he rose upon his legs
his head could be seen above a hill.
He shook the earth when he ran,
and when he drank at a spring
no water was left for the people.
He roamed the plains in search of food
and when he found a tribe
he ate them all
and that tribe was gone for ever.
There was no place to hide from the Whowie,
for there was no place in which he could not go.

Then the tribes found a small valley,
and the way into this valley
was through a narrow gorge.
The Whowie could not walk through this gorge
for he was wider than the space between the walls.

The Water Rat tribe,
those that were left
after the Whowie had attacked them,
passed through this gorge
and rested there while they planned
how to destroy this monster.

They sent up smoke signals
to summon all the tribes
and the people of the tribes saw the signals
and came to the valley for a council.

They marched as to battle.
The bravest of the warriors
led their people through the gorge,
then came the elders,
and behind them the tribespeople,
dancing and shouting.

When all the tribes
were assembled
the Water Rat people told them
the Whowie must die.
If the Whowie lived
all people would vanish from the earth
and there would be no knowledge of the earth
in any mind.
The tribes decided
to select the best warriors of those that were there
and these warriors were to follow the Whowie
till they destroyed it.

Then the warriors who were selected
bade goodbye to their people
and left the valley through the narrow gorge.
For many days
they roamed the country
searching for the Whowie's tracks.
Then they found them.
Each footprint was the length of a man
and was pressed the width of a hand into the earth.
The warriors knew
that it was the custom
of the Whowie to retreat
to a cave after it had fed.

There it slept
till it became hungry again.
The warriors did not know
the whereabouts of this cave,
but they followed the Whowie's tracks
and the tracks led them
to its lair in the mountains.

The warriors stood at the entrance
and peered in,
but the darkness in the cave
was blacker than the night
and they could not see the Whowie.
Then the Whowie moved in the darkness
and they heard
the rustle and scrape of its scales upon the rock.
A smell of death came out upon them
and they moved back to escape it.

They talked together,
then decided
to build a huge fire
inside the entrance to the cave
so that the heat and smoke
would drive the Whowie out.
So they built a fire
of logs and branches
and packed it with dried leaves.
When they fired it
the flames leaped up to the height of the roof.
Then they threw water upon it
and smoke and steam filled the cave.

They heard the Whowie roar,
then the rumble of its feet.
It flung itself through the fire,
and the flames and smoke
hid it from sight.

Then it plunged
on to the grass
where the warriors awaited it.
But its eyes were closed
with the smoke
and it could not see.
The warriors leaped upon it
with their spears and nulla-nullas.
They climbed upon it
and speared down;
they ran beneath it
and speared up.
The Whowie
flung itself against trees in its pain
and the trees fell,
but the warriors were always upon it
thrusting with their spears,
and its blood ran through the grass.
Then it fell and died.

The warriors returned
to the valley
and told the people
that the Whowie had gone for ever.
The people danced and sang,
then left the valley and returned to their camps.
And animals that eat men were never seen again.

How the red dust came to blow

The red dust that hides the sun
did not always blow over the land.
In the Dreamtime there was no dust,
and rain was never withheld from the earth.

Darana, the spirit man,
lived in those days.
He was the first of the rain-makers.
He studied the insects
and the birds.
He watched the ants
carrying their eggs
up the trunks of trees
where they hid them
behind shreds of bark
so that they would be out of reach
when flood waters covered the land.

He gathered the white gypsum
that crumbles in the dry weather
and swells with moisture
when rain is approaching.

When Darana wanted rain
he took a wooden dish
and filled it with pieces of gypsum.
He placed it upon the ground
and two tribesmen chanted over it.
Then he made
a tall framework of wood
upon which he painted his totem
and the wavy lines of water.
He called this frame a kandri.

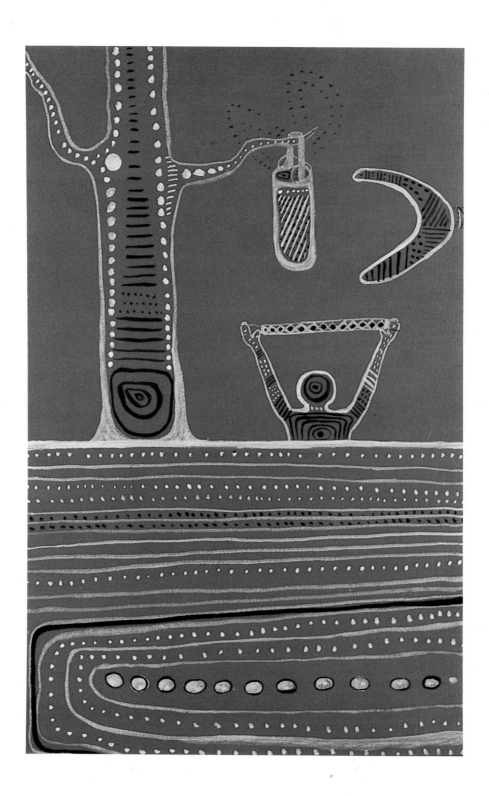

He placed the kandri upon his shoulders
and chanted and danced
until the clouds came over
and poured their rain upon the earth.

One day,
Darana brought so much rain from the sky
that water spread all over the country
and the rivers bore the trunks of trees
along with them in their rush.
The water rose to Darana's waist,
but he stayed where he was.
The tribespeople fled to higher ground
and when they were safe
Darana waded to the place where the rivers rise
and where all the wild water had gathered
for its journey to the sea.

Here he placed his kandri in the ground.
He chanted over it and danced
and the rain ceased
and the waters flowed away.
The rivers grew quiet
and the sun shone brightly once again.

Then grass and flowers and trees grew as never before.
The trails were blocked with vines,
and plants grew among rocks and over sandy places.
The witchetty grubs came in such numbers
that the tribes could not eat all they gathered.
They lay the grubs on sheets of bark
and dried them in the sun.
They filled their dilly bags with dried grubs
and hung their dilly bags in the trees
so that this food would be available
when the plague had gone.
Darana was pleased to see this store of food
and he asked the tribes to treasure it.

One day a boy found one of these dilly bags
and he threw his boomerang at it.
The boomerang hit the dilly bag
and the dilly bag burst into a cloud of red dust
that covered the land and hid the sun.
The tribespeople were afraid,
for they knew that Darana would be angered
and might punish them.

Then they heard
the voice of Darana
and he told them what to do.
They ran back to their camp
and gathered pieces of gypsum.
They covered the stones
with emu fat and feathers
so that no gypsum could be seen.
If ever these stones
were scratched or broken
the red dust would come again
and all the tribes would die of starvation.

The blue crane

There was once a woman
who had three sons.
Eurowie was a great dancer and jumper,
Pithowie was a hunter,
but Koolatowie, the youngest,
was loved by the people
even though he did not possess
the gifts of his brothers.

The two elder brothers were jealous of Koolatowie
and refused to teach him how to dance and hunt.
They were proud
of their prowess in these things
and were afraid of a rival.

But the elders of the tribe
saw some greatness in Koolatowie
and they taught him
the customs and laws of the tribe
with a thoroughness
they did not give to others.
They took him with them on the hunt
and they revealed to him
the secrets of tracking.

Soon Koolatowie could
distinguish the tracks of any animal or bird,
and he developed into a great hunter.

When he was initiated into the tribe
he did not cry out at the pain,
nor did he show fear
when dread secrets were revealed to him.

Because of this
the hatred of the brothers grew,
and at length the old men banished them
to another tribe
where it was thought
they could do Koolatowie no harm.
The brothers were enraged at this expulsion,
and on their way to the camp of the tribe
with whom they had to live,
they drove all the game before them.
They traversed the hunting grounds
of their people
from end to end,
frightening the emus and kangaroos
with wild shouting.
They set fire to the grass
so that mobs of kangaroos
fled in panic
and emus sped through the scrub
seeking safety on distant plains.

This, the brothers did
to discredit Koolatowie
as a hunter,
for they knew his people were dependent
on his skill for food
and now he would return
empty-handed from the chase.

The three brothers
had an uncle called Chirr-bookie.
He was a good man
and he loved Koolatowie, the youngest, as a son.
He was one of the elders
who had trained Koolatowie in the hunt.
The country over which they hunted,
and on which his tribe lived
was his country by decree.

Now his country was bereft of game,
and each day Koolatowie returned
without a kangaroo or an emu for the tribe.
All the game had fled, he said,
nor did he know why this was so.

One day,
Eurowie and Pithowie sneaked into Chirr-bookie's country
and released an emu there,
then they waited.
Koolatowie, out hunting,
found its tracks and followed them.
Soon he came upon the bird and killed it.
His two brothers had followed him,
and when Koolatowie saw them
they put down their spears and woomeras
in a gesture of friendship.
Koolatowie, too, placed his weapons on the ground.
Then he walked up to them
so that they might talk together.
When they had greeted each other
the two elder brothers
suddenly fell upon Koolatowie
and killed him with their hands.
Then they returned to their camp.

Chirr-bookie, their uncle,
was troubled when Koolatowie failed
to return from the hunt.
He set off to look for him,
then finding his tracks,
followed them until he came upon his body
lying hidden in the grass.
Chirr-bookie knew who had done this thing.
The tracks of Eurowie and Pithowie
were plain on the ground
and these he followed
till he came to their camp.

He greeted them as friends,
not revealing that he knew
they had slain their brother.
When night came,
Chirr-bookie asked for a mia-mia
away from those of the brothers.
He was tired from the hunt, he said,
and wanted to sleep in quietness.

Late in the night he rose
and crept silently to the mia-mias
of the two brothers and their wives.
He thrust a firestick
into the dry leaves that covered them
and they burnt furiously.
Eurowie and Pithowie were burnt
with their mia-mias
and with them
their wives and children.

Chirr-bookie returned to his camp,
but his head was bowed
and he saw no beauty on the earth.

Then the spirits of his Dreaming
came to him in the night
and they breathed upon him
and he became a blue crane,
a bird like a spear
whose wings have strength and beauty.

Why the tribes speak different languages

There was a time
when all the tribes spoke the one tongue.
Every man understood what the stranger said
and no man stumbled over strange words
or was thought foolish in the silence that comes
when the one cannot speak to the other.
There were many tribes
and there was one language,
thus knowledge passed easily between them
and friendship bound tribe to tribe.

But the marriage laws
that forbade those of one tribe
from marrying those of another
caused dissatisfaction among them,
so the old men met
and then announced that the members of all tribes
could intermarry.
A Dingo man could marry
a Goanna woman;
a Kangaroo woman could marry
an Emu man;
and so on through all the tribes.

But some tribes were angry
at this change in the law.
They refused to accept the ruling of the old men
and they sharpened their spears
and stood their ground.
And the people that were angered the most
were those of the Tortoise,
the Frog,
and the Crow tribes.

Then the old men called a meeting of the tribes
so that the matter could be discussed between them.
But those in favour of the change
had no faith in the meeting.
They prepared for an attack from
the Tortoise,
the Frog,
and the Crow tribes,
for these people were warriors.
They brought forth their boomerangs,
their nulla-nullas and their spears,
and they waited.
But the men of
the Tortoise,
the Frog,
and the Crow tribes
knew that they were outnumbered,
and they made a plan
whereby the tribes
who favoured the changing of the law
would fight between themselves
and thus be destroyed.

When all the tribes were together
on the day arranged,
the Tortoise,
the Frog,
and the Crow people
started to sing and dance.
When one tired
another took his place.
They pounded the earth and shouted,
nor would they stop
when it was customary that all should eat.
Those that watched them
did not leave the corroboree ground,
for to do so in the midst of singing and dancing
would have brought evil happenings upon them.

So they stayed
and their hunger grew and grew,
and their limbs ached
and their eyes grew heavy in their heads.
For three days
the Tortoise
and Crow
and Frog people
danced and sang,
and on the third day
the hunger and fatigue
of those who watched
made these tribesmen irritable and bitter-tongued.
They spoke angrily to each other
and men struck their friends
The common tongue
made all understand the insults that were shouted
from one tribesman to another,
and anger grew to rage,
so that the people rose to their feet
and fought together.
And the fighting between friends
was more terrible
than the fighting between enemies.
Many were slain
and the tribes parted in hate.

Then each tribe
resolved that they would never again
speak the language of other tribes.
Each tribe created a language of its own
so that what they said was for themselves alone.
And thus it is today.

How fire began

When the world was young, men were without fire.
Game was plentiful, but it was eaten raw
and there was little pleasure in the eating.

One day, a Water Rat man was gnawing
a piece of hard wood and a spark flew from his mouth
and fell on the dry grass.
The grass burst into flame.
The Water Rat man was astonished.
He threw wood upon the flames to stifle them,
but the wood caught fire and burnt with a great heat.
A snake that was hidden in the wood
was roasted by the flames
and the smell of its cooked flesh was so pleasing
to the Water Rat man that he ate it and it was good.
The Water Rat man kept feeding the fire
so that it would not go out,
and soon all the tribesmen heard of this wonder
and they came to see it.
They discovered they could carry a firestick
and start other fires.
So firesticks were carried across the land,
and there was a fire in the camp of every tribe.

For many years the fires were preserved
so that no man shivered at night
nor ate raw meat after the hunt.
The people grew lazy
and slept far more than they did when they were cold.

One year a great storm swept over the land.
The rain did not come in drops,
but came like water poured from a gourd.

All the fires were extinguished and the people again
shivered at night and ate raw meat,
for they had forgotten, in their laziness,
how to rekindle the fires that were gone.

It was at this time that an Eaglehawk man
took two Snake women for his wives.
They were thin women with still eyes
and they loved the hot sun and dreaded the cold.
When their husband was out hunting
they would bask in the sun,
lying on the sand without movement till he returned.
In the bush near their camp was an old ant-hill.
It was sheltered from the wind
and was hidden from sight amongst the trees.
Here the sun shone with great strength
and the two wives often went there
and lay with their backs propped
against the grass and clay that formed the mound.
No one knew where they had gone,
since they were secretive women and never talked
about their visits to this warm place in the bush.

One day,
the heat of the sun and the protection of their bodies
ignited the grass in the ant-hill and it smouldered,
then began to burn with a red glow.
At first the wives were afraid,
then they were pleased that this thing had happened.
They were the only ones who knew
of the presence of fire in the world
and this knowledge filled them with power.
When their husband returned from the hunt
they were back at the camp,
and when he gave them their share
of the meat he had brought
they did not eat it but waited till he slept
then crept back to the ant-hill.

There they took a stick
and uncovered the fire
burning in the centre of the ant-hill,
and into the hole they made
they thrust the meat their husband had given them.
When it was cooked
they took it out and ate it,
then returned to the camp.
Each day they did this till the Eaglehawk man,
their husband, became suspicious.
He could smell cooked meat
and he guessed that his wives
had discovered the secret of making a fire.
Yet, when he questioned them, they denied it.
He tried to track them
when they disappeared into the bush,
but the wives knew
that he would do this
and they concealed their tracks with great skill.
When he asked them
what they did when they went into the bush
they told him they were searching for yams.

The Eaglehawk man was troubled
and he visited the neighbouring tribes
and told them of his wives' behaviour
and asked them
to help him discover the reason
why they ate cooked meat,
though denying that they had ever seen a fire.
So the tribes, in turn,
tried to catch the wives cooking meat at a fire,
but the wives were crafty and always eluded them.
They would never visit the ant-hill when men were near,
and when they wished to cook their meat
they walked many miles
so that they could approach the ant-hill
from the opposite direction to the camp.

Then a man of the Lizard tribe said
he would discover the secret
if he were allowed to work alone.
The tribes agreed to this
and the Lizard man went into the bush
and lay concealed there for many days.
He did not join his brothers in the hunt
nor return to his camp when darkness fell,
so that the two wives concluded
he had gone on a long journey.
One day, all the tribesmen pretended to go hunting.
When they had disappeared
the two wives took their meat
and walked to the ant-hill
confident that there was no one to see them.
But the Lizard man followed them
and when they reached the ant-hill
and began uncovering the fire
he crept up on the opposite side
and thrust a firestick deep into the mound.
When he withdrew it,
it was aflame,
and he gave a shout of triumph
and bore the burning firestick back to the camp
where the tribesmen were waiting for him.

The two wives were seized with a great fury
at the successful ruse of the Lizard man.
They swore vengeance
and there by the ant-hill they turned into snakes,
so that from then on they could attack all men.

And now
snakes strike at all those who venture near them,
and if they touch such people,
these people die in pain.

64

The Eaglehawk
and the Crow

When the dark people first came to live on the earth
they formed themselves into tribes.
The tribes kept to the land allotted them
and did not interfere with each other.
Then men of each tribe
married the girls of their own tribe.
The women of one tribe
could not marry the men of another tribe,
nor were they allowed to speak to these men.
This was the law.

In these days the Crow tribe had few men
that a woman would desire.
The Crow men were old and slow in hunting.
One Crow man had a daughter whom he loved,
and so that she might rear sons of courage
he gave her in marriage to an Eaglehawk man
who was famed for his valour.
The tribes were angry at this breaking of the law,
but the Eaglehawk man was a warrior
and they were afraid to oppose him.

The daughter of the Crow man was happy with her husband,
but he was often away hunting,
and gradually she grew discontented.
She was always restless when he was away and,
at these times, she looked with favour at other men.
One day, the Eaglehawk man returned from the hunt
and found his wife talking to a man of the Magpie tribe.
He fell into a rage at the sight,
for though he had broken the law in his marriage
he abided by the law in other things.
And he was a jealous man.

65

Thereafter he refused to get food for his wife,
nor would he allow others to feed her.
So she became thin and weak,
and when her first-born arrived,
she died among the women.
And if it had not been for her hunger
she would have lived.
The Eaglehawk man, her husband,
took his son and gave him to another woman to rear,
and his love for this son was great.

The brother of the Eaglehawk man's wife,
a Crow man,
heard of his sister's death and he swore to avenge her.
He bided his time
and when the baby had grown
and could play with other children
he saw how greatly the Eaglehawk man loved the child,
and he decided to kill it
so that the suffering of the Eaglehawk man
would be as great as that of his sister.

One day he approached the camp of the Eaglehawk man,
staggering as if with the fatigue of a long journey,
and holding his arm as if he had been injured in the chase.
The Eaglehawk man welcomed him and bade him rest.
He gave him food, and the Crow man ate,
then lay beneath a tree as if exhausted.
He stayed there for three days.
On the third day
the Eaglehawk man went hunting
and the Crow man was left alone with the child.
Then he rose and killed the child,
and around the place where he had killed him
he trampled the grass
and pounded the bare patches until dust arose
and the earth was disturbed as if by many feet.

When the father returned
the Crow man told him that a marauding tribe
had killed his son
and that he had routed them and driven them away.
The Eaglehawk man was grief-stricken
and could not speak.

Next day he searched the trampled earth
looking for footprints
that would tell him what men had done this deed.
But the footprints were all the same
and they were the footprints of the Crow man.
Then the Eaglehawk man knew,
but he remained silent
and next day
he invited the Crow man to go hunting with him
and they set off together towards the hills.
At the foot of the hills
they came on two kangaroos feeding.
The kangaroos saw them and bounded away,
but the Crow man had raised his spear
and was just about to hurl it at the fleeing animals
when the Eaglehawk man attacked him from behind,
bringing his nulla-nulla down with such force
on the Crow man's head
that he killed him.

When he knew he was dead he rested awhile
and thought of his son,
then he dragged the Crow man's body back to his camp
and buried him beneath the ground.
By the time he had done this it was night,
and he lay down to sleep.
But no sooner had he closed his eyes
than lightning flashed
and thunder rumbled among the hills.
A storm came down upon him
and thunder shook the earth upon which he crouched.

67

Lightning struck again and again
at the grave of the Crow man,
and above the noise of the thunder
he could hear the shouts of the Crow man
go past him on the wind.
And he was afraid
because he knew that the Crow man
had taken the lightning for his totem,
and the Crow man's spirit was seeking revenge.

The Eaglehawk man fled
from place to place seeking shelter,
but the lightning followed him
with spears of flame
so that his flesh was seared with the heat.
At last, exhausted,
he flung himself beneath a ledge of rock
and when he had done this
all the thunder moved in upon him
in one mighty sound above him.
A shaft of lightning leapt forth,
shattering the ledge of rock beneath which he sheltered
and consuming the Eaglehawk man in a burst of light.
And out of the light,
as from a nest,
flew an Eaglehawk.
It rose into the night sky and was gone.
Then from the grave of the Crow man
a crow flew forth,
a bird singed coal-black by lightning.

Next day the Eaglehawk and the crow
were seen by the tribes
and it was the first time these birds had lived.

The selfish ones

There was once a tribe
whose country lay many miles from the sea.

Kangaroos, wallabies and koalas were plentiful
in the bush where these people roamed,
but they became tired
of eating the game that fell to their spears
and longed for a different food.
'We will go to the sea,' said one.
'In the sea there are many fish.'

So the tribe marched through the forest
until they came to the sea,
and they came to the sea at Shaving Point
where there are lakes and lagoons near the sea's edge.
And in all these waters there were fish.

On that summer evening when the tribe arrived,
the insects were thick above the grass and the water,
and the slap of leaping fish could be heard in the camp.
The men were excited
at the thought of all the fish they would catch.
The women talked happily one to another.
They carried their babies
to where the spent waves slip up the sand,
so that the little ones
could feel the first touch
of the blue water that was salt to the taste
and stretched to the world's edge.
The men made fishing nets and traps.
They waded into the shallows
and speared the fish
that lurked just beneath the surface.

When they hurled their spears
they plunged forward to grasp their catch,
then they would hold it aloft for all to see.

With these people, on their journey to the sea,
had come their dogs.
These dogs were strong and fleet
and had once been men.
They lived on the game they pursued and caught,
since the few scraps tossed to them by the men and women
would not have kept them alive.
In the home country of the tribe
the dogs were never short of food,
for kangaroos and wallabies were plentiful
and the dogs were good hunters.
But in this new camp by the sea
there were only fish to eat
and the dogs were hungry, for they could not catch fish.

One day,
the men returned to the camp with so many fish
that their backs were bowed beneath the catch.
They piled them in a silver heap near the campfire
and lay beneath the trees to rest
while the women cooked them.

The dogs looked at this gleaming heap
and their hunger became more than they could bear.
The leader of the dogs walked over to the men
and said, 'Give us some fish to eat.
You have more that you need, and we are hungry.'
'Go way, dog,' shouted one of the men.
'Dogs don't eat fish.'
'We will eat fish,' said the dog.
'There are no kangaroos here for us to eat
and we are thin with hunger.
Give us some of the fish
so that we might eat and become strong again.'

'Go and catch some fish if you wish to eat,'
said another man.
'These are our fish
and we will not share them with dogs.'
'Dogs cannot catch fish,' said the dog.
'Then you can starve,' said the first man,
and he threw a stone at the dog.

Then all the men rose
and they drove the dogs from the camp
with sticks and stones,
and they shouted and jeered at them as they fled.
The dogs ran deep into the bush
and there they made a camp
and talked and talked and talked.

Back in the camp of the tribe
the men and women feasted
till only the bones of the fish were left.
Of all their catch not a fish remained.
They had eaten them all.
They sat there talking until the moon had risen,
and when the moon had risen
the dogs returned to the camp
and they were filled with anger.

Then the leader of the dogs left the other dogs
and he cried out and raced through the camp,
and he leaped as he raced
and there was fire on his feet.
'This for all selfish people,' he cried,
and he threw his magic over the camp
and it went over the camp like a wind
and all the people that were in that camp,
the women and the children and the men,
turned to stone.
And selfish people from then on had hearts of stone
and no warmth or kindness was in them.

How the moon came

After the islands came up from the deep sea,
trees grew thickly upon them.
On some islands the sea water was trapped in hollows
and became saltwater lagoons.
In these lagoons were many fish.

At this time there lived two sisters
called Nakari and Kurramara
and they went to Bribie Island to look for food.
Nakari had a baby
and she carried it upon her shoulders.
Bribie Island was young,
and the new trees had no tracks between them.
The sisters got lost among the trees
and could not find the way.
They walked till they came to the centre of the island
where the grass trees are.
Near the grass trees was a saltwater lagoon.
'We will camp here,' said Nakari.
'This is a good place.'
She laid the baby upon some paper bark and it slept.

The sisters built a mia-mia of bark
then they went to the lagoon to spear fish.
They caught a big fish
different to all other fish.
It was round like the moon
and shadowed as the moon is shadowed.
They carried it back to their camp
and made a fire on which to cook it.
They waited till the flames had burnt the wood to coals
then they placed the fish on the coals
and covered it with ashes.

74

'This is a big fish,' said Kurramara.
'It will take a long time to cook.
While it is cooking we will look for yams.'

The sisters took their yam sticks
and walked into the bush
where the yam vines encircled the trunks of trees
and the bright green leaves hung down from the branches.
They filled their dilly bags with yams
then returned to the camp.
Nakari hurried over to the fire
for she was hungry.
She looked at the ashes and the coals
then cried out to Kurramara:
'Sister, come here.
Our fish has gone.'

Kurramara came to her
and together they looked at the ashes,
which were scattered round the fire,
and at the coals, that had been thrown aside.
Then they saw a pathway of ashes
leading away from the fire,
a pathway made from the ashes that fell from the fish
as it escaped.

Kurramara and Nakari, the two sisters,
followed the trail of ashes through the trees.
They followed it
till it ended at the foot of a tall bloodwood tree.
'The fish will be here,' said Kurramara.
'There is no track away from this tree.'
They looked up the tree
and there was the fish
halfway up the trunk.
'Sister, run back to the camp
and get our spears and yam sticks,' said Kurramara.
'I will watch the fish while you are gone.'

Nakari ran back to the camp
and Kurramara stayed.
She threw sticks at the fish
but it climbed higher
and she could not hit it.
When Nakari returned
the sisters tried to spear the fish
but it moved higher and higher up the trunk.
They threw their yam sticks at it
but it moved higher than they could throw.

Nakari was hungry and she began to cry.
'Sister, one of us should have stayed at the fire
and watched that fish
then it would not have got away.
Now we have only yams to eat
and we are hungry.'
'When the fish climbs higher into the branches
they will break and it will fall,' said Kurramara.
'We will wait.'
They waited all that day till night came
and when darkness filled the tree
the fish leaped from the branches
and moved westward across the sky like a light.

The sisters returned to the camp
and next morning they walked
till they came to the beach.
Nakari laid her baby on the sand
and covered it with a rug of possum skins
while she and Kurramara looked for shell-fish.
They walked from rock to rock,
and while they were away
the tide came in
and the big waves
curved over the baby and fell upon it.
And the sand washed up by the waves
covered the baby till only a foot lay in the sea.

When the sisters returned,
Nakari saw the foot and she cried out
and uncovered the baby,
but it was dead.
The sisters buried the baby on the beach
and went away
but Nakari looked back many times as they walked.
Then she stopped
and Kurramara took her by the hand
and led her,
and after that she did not look back again.

On and on they walked
till they reached the channel
between the island and the mainland
and across the channel was Caloundra.
Together they swam across the channel
and found some caves along the shore.
That night they slept in one of the caves
and next morning they followed the beach
till they came to Mooloolah Heads.
They swam the passage and reached Maroochy Beach.

Across the water from the beach
was an island called Mudjimba.
The sisters stood and looked at it
and suddenly an enormous log grew from the air
and stretched across the sea from the beach to the island.
Nakari and Kurramara walked across the log
and when they stepped on to the island
the log vanished.
They stood on the island and there was no way back.

'How do you like this place, sister?' asked Kurramara.
'We will live here now for ever.
We will never get back again.
This is our place now.
We can never swim back.'

'I like this place
if there is food in this place,'
said Nakari.
'I would like to live here for ever.
What will we eat in this place?'
'We will eat bread-fruit and fish and crabs and yams,'
said Kurramara.
'There is plenty of food in this place.'
They lit a fire and sat before it for they were tired.
The smoke from the fire did not blow upon them
but rose into the air and tied them to the sky.

Then night came
and they looked up and saw the moon.
'Oh! look, sister, there is the fish we caught!'
cried Nakari.
They both watched the moon
and they both felt sad
that this biggest of all fish had escaped them.

Next night they watched it again and it was smaller,
as if someone were eating it.
And each night it was eaten away
until there was only half a fish,
until there was only a quarter of a fish,
until there was only the round edge of the fish left.
The next night after that there was nothing.
'It is all eaten,' said Kurramara. 'Our fish is gone.'

And now,
on all the moonlight nights for ever,
the sisters sit
and watch their fish being eaten away.
And the smoke of their campfire, curling upwards,
can always be seen by day,
though they are like the air
through which you can walk and not know it is there.

The Bittern
who caught a dugong

When the Bittern was a man
he set a net and caught a dugong.
It was a very big dugong
so he tied it to his canoe
and towed it behind him in the water.
'I will have fun with my friends,'
the Bittern said to himself.
'I will make my friends work hard
for a piece of this dugong.'

When he reached the beach
he called all his friends and said,
'I have caught a dugong.
You follow me in your canoes
and we will eat this dugong in a good place.'
So all his friends pushed their canoes into the water
and followed the Bittern as he paddled along the shore.
'The Bittern is a kind man,' they said.
'When he catches a dugong, we all have dugong.'

The Bittern kept on paddling
till he came to Russell Island.
'This is a good place, Russell Island,'
he said to his friends. 'We will camp here.'
His friends were pleased
that the feast was soon to begin.
They alighted from their canoes
and made a camp on the island
then they said to the Bittern,
'Bring the dugong in from the water
so that the feast can begin.'
'No, this is not a good place,' said the Bittern.
'I just see this is a bad place. You follow me further.'

So all the friends got into their canoes again
and followed the Bittern till they came to Coochimudlo.
They gathered round the Bittern's canoe and said,
'This very good camping place.
Good for eating dugong.'
'No, we go further,' said the Bittern.
'Better places further.'

So, with the dugong still in the water,
the Bittern paddled on
and his friends followed him in their canoes.
But now they didn't talk so much
about that fellow, Bittern.
They were quiet
from the heavy work of the paddling.
After awhile they reached Peel Island
and the Bittern let his canoe drift
while he looked at the beach.
'This is a very good place,' said his friends.
'We eat dugong here, eh?'
'This bad place,' said the Bittern.
'We go more further.'

The friends followed him in their canoes
till they came to Green Island.
'Ah!' said his friends. 'Best place, here.
Good for eating dugong.'
'No, this is bad place,' said the Bittern.
'We find better place further.'
'When that dugong be cooked?' asked his friends.
'We go too many furthers.'
'I catch that dugong in my net,' said the Bittern.
'It is my dugong
and I cook it for my friends in a good place.'

So they all set off once more
with the dugong still in the water.
They paddled till they came to St Helena.

'This, best place of all,' said the Bittern's friends.
'Now we pull our canoes on beach, eh?'
But the Bittern shook his head and looked sad.
'I'm sorry, my friends; this place worst place of all.
We go to Mud Island and eat dugong on Mud Island.
It is a very good place.'

They set off again and the friends were so tired
that the Bittern reached Mud Island before them.
'You are slow, my friends,'
he called out from the beach when they arrived.
'You do not like dugong, eh?'
Then one of his friends,
the strongest of them all, said,
'Before we say we like dugong,
is this the furtherest place?'
'Yes,' said the Bittern.
'We will pull the dugong on the beach and have a feast.'
When they had dragged the dugong on the beach
they cut it up and lit a big fire
and cooked the meat on the fire.

Now, on this island was an old woman
who lived in the air over that place
and on the ground of that place
and in the sea round that place.
Sometimes people saw her
and sometimes no one saw her,
but they knew she was there.
When the dugong meat began to cook,
she sniffed the air and said,
'There must be something nice over there.
I'll go and see.'
She walked through the trees till she came to the fire,
then she said to the Bittern and his friends,
'Hello, my grandchildren.
I'm living here and am hungry.
Give me food.'

They gave her some meat
and she placed it on a stone and said,
'I will get my dilly bag to carry this meat.'
After she had done this
she went and hid among the trees
to plan how she could get all that dugong.

When she had gone, the Bittern said,
'That old woman will take all our meat.
This is a bad place. We will go further.'
They gathered all the meat
and packed it in the canoes
then paddled away from the beach,
but the old woman came back
before they were far from the land
and she ran out into the water screaming at them.
She slapped the water with the palms of her hands
and made waves
that rolled towards the canoes with foaming heads.
The waves went over the canoes and they sank
and the Bittern and his friends
were thrown in the water.
The dugong meat fell out of the canoes and floated away
and each separate piece of meat became a dugong
and the dugong swam
among the men and the women in the sea.

The Bittern and his friends were carried by the waves
like mangrove leaves.
The white of the waves tossed them and covered them
and threw them out again
until they were cast on a far beach
where they lay in the sun till strength came to them.
Then they looked back over the sea towards Mud Island
and they had never seen so many dugong before.

The girl
who made dilly bags

In a land
where the mountains and sea were brothers
and the trees were straight and tall,
there lived a young girl called Lowana
who was shy with people.

She liked quiet things and quiet places.
Her eyes were dark and timid
but when she walked alone through the bush
they became bright with the wonder that she felt.
She lived alone
in a mia-mia of bark
and made dilly bags
for those who needed them.
Her fingers were long
and they plaited the strands of string
with quick movements,
so that the number of dilly bags she made
was greater than that of any other woman.

Because of her quietness
few spoke for long with her.
The young men of her tribe
passed her by on their way to the hunt,
for she had no laughing words to exchange with them
nor any gesture that would make them stay.
Yet, because of one young man
who strode with them,
she would watch them go
till they disappeared
among the trees,
and after they had gone
she was lonelier than before.

The name of this man was Yoadi.

At a distant place
there was to be a feast
and all the tribes gathered to go.

The children ran across the grass
and between the trees
and shouted at each other.
Women lifted babies upon their shoulders
and laughed together.
They slung dilly bags upon their backs,
the dilly bags Lowana had made.
They took their yam sticks
and the men took their spears
and woomeras
and they moved away,
the men and women of all the tribes together.

They walked one behind the other
and when the leading men were hidden from sight,
people were still moving from the camp
with no more than the length of an arm between them.

Soon only Lowana was left
for no one had thought to say,
'Walk with us to the feast.'
They had forgotten her.
Her mother and her father
and all her relations had gone
and they did not miss her.
She was too quiet to be missed
when people walked together with laughter.

The tribes walked for many days
and after they passed a place,
there was no game left at that place,
for there were many to feed.

When ten days had gone
Yoadi walked back from the lead
till he reached the last old woman
and the last tired child.
Then he called out
and all the people stopped
and he demanded of them,
'Where is Lowana?'
and there was none could answer him.
And from the oldest woman
at the end of the line of people
to the men who led the way,
there travelled the words,
'She is not here.'
And the words came back
from the leading men to Yoadi
and when they reached him
he trembled.

'I will return for her,' he said.
'She will be hungry.'
So he took his stone axe,
his spear,
his woomera,
his shield
and his nulla-nulla
and he left them.

He set off along the track they had traversed
and because the game had gone,
his hunting took him far from the track
to places where the way was hard.
He cut footholds in the possum trees
and carried his kill across his shoulder.
He gathered sugar bag
from the bee hives in hollow limbs
and each day
he walked till darkness came.

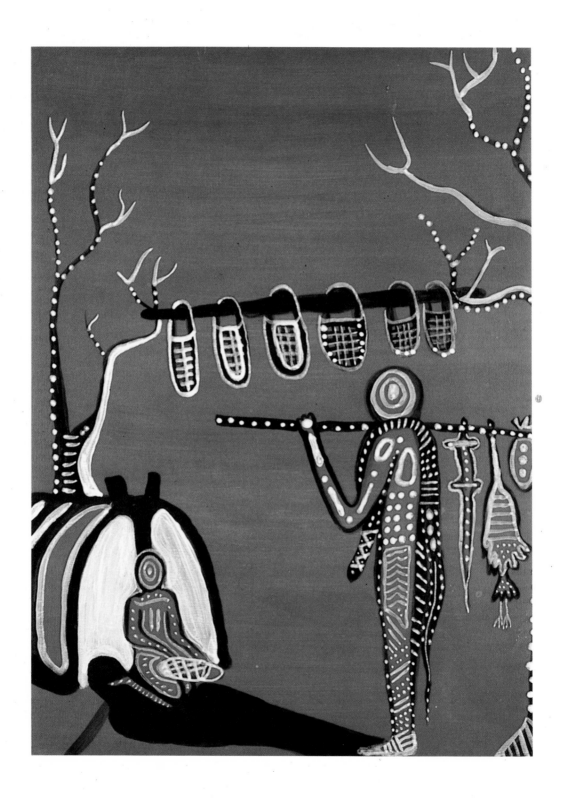

The closer he got to Lowana's mia-mia
the longer were the stages he walked,
though he staggered from the weight of food
he was bringing her.

She had sat in her mia-mia
since the tribe had gone,
her fingers busy making dilly bags.
The food she gathered
did not satisfy her hunger.
She had no spears to hunt for game.
She lived on yams
and water-lily roots
and shell-fish she gathered on the beach

One day
the string
she used for the dilly bags
kept breaking,
she made mistakes in plaiting,
and her fingers fumbled in their work.
She became confused
and troubled
because of her clumsiness.
She plaited with greater care,
pulled the strings together without jerking them.
But she knew why her fingers shook,
why she kept looking towards the bush
where the tall trees stood silently waiting.
Someone was coming nearer
and nearer
and nearer.
She could feel the quickening of her heart.
She lowered her head
so that all she could see was the dilly bag in her hands.
Someone was coming nearer and nearer.
She clutched the bag with fingers that could not move.
Someone was coming nearer.

She would not lift her head.
Then his shadow fell over her and she looked up at him.
She saw his face above her
then her eyes closed
and she fell to the ground and lay still.

Yoadi knelt beside her
and lifted her head on his arm.
He held her
and watched her face
without moving
and without speaking.
After awhile
she opened her eyes
and looked at him
and there was no fear in them.
'What is the matter?' he asked.
'What you come for?'
'I come for you.'
'What for?'
'You belong to me.
Your father and mother promise you to me a long time ago.
I come now.'
She lay watching him.
'Are you hungry?' he asked.
'Yes,' she replied.
He gave her the food he had brought for her
and watched her while she ate.

'We will go now,' he said when she had finished.
'We will go, join our people.'
'Yes,' she said.
He walked down the track
and she followed him.
She left her mia-mia
and all her dilly bags
and she never looked back.
She saw only the man ahead of her.

90

The rainbow and
the bread-fruit flower

On Peel Island, long ago, there lived three brothers
called Walara, Nabijura and Kurramon.
Walara and Nabijura were strong and handsome;
Kurramon was weak and thin.

They all loved the same girl
and each wanted her for a wife,
but she would not say which one she favoured.
Her name was Lamari and she lived alone.
Walara and Nabijura decided to bring her food
so that she would know they were kindly men
who would make good husbands.
Then, when each had brought her food,
she could choose between them
and they agreed that the one she chose
would not suffer the anger of the other.
First, Walara brought her fish from the sea,
but she would not be his wife,
then Nabijura brought her game from the bush,
but neither would she be his wife.
Then, Kurramon, the brother who was thin and weak,
said he would try also,
but the handsome brothers mocked him
and called him names.
'She will never be your wife,' they said,
and they walked away from him, laughing.

Kurramon walked into the bush
and gathered fruit so that he, too,
could bring food to Lamari.
He caught fish and speared a kangaroo,
so the food he gathered
was more than that of his brothers.

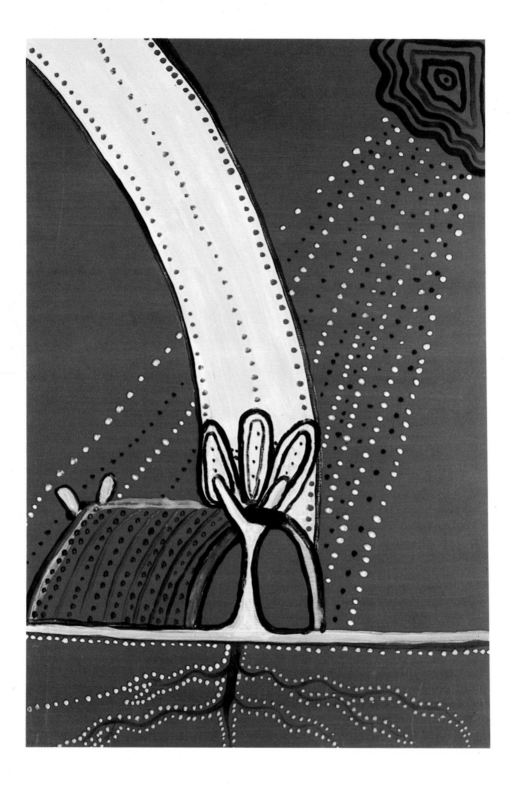

Before he took this gift to Lamari,
he walked to his mother's grave
and it was fourteen days since she died.
He placed his hands on the earth that covered her
and the strength of his mother passed into him
and he became big and strong like his brothers.
Then he went to Lamari with the food he gathered
and asked her to be his wife.
She rose and went with him for she loved him.

He took her to a secret place in the bush
so that his brothers would not know she was his wife.
When he visited his brothers
he did not speak of her
nor did he take her with him when he came their way.
But the brothers suspected him, and,
when they saw him taking food into the bush,
they followed him.
They hid behind a tree and
watched him give the food to his wife
and they saw by her face that she loved him.
Because of this they hated him,
and, thereafter, they sought ways to kill him.

When they hunted with him
they moved so that he stood between them
and the game they wished to spear,
and when they threw their spears
it was at him they aimed them.
But he was quick to move
and no spear ever harmed him.
He watched his brothers always and they knew this.
They hoped that he might trust them again
and in order that this might be so
they offered to build him a mia-mia
that would turn the heavy rain
or give shade when the sun was hot.
Kurramon worked with them and they built a mia-mia.

93

When it was finished
Walara and Nabijura asked him
to go fishing with them on the reef.
He agreed to go though he knew
they would attempt to kill him out on the sea.

Before he went with his brothers to the reef
he visited Lamari and told her of his fears.
Then he said to her,
'If my brothers kill me a little bird will come to you
with a drop of blood on its bill
and when you see it, you will know I am dead.'
When she heard this, all strength left Lamari
and she could not speak.
Then Kurramon went away from her to his brothers
and they sailed out to the reef.
The brothers paddled the canoe
to where a giant clam lay on the reef,
then they said to Kurramon,
'You dive in with your spear and bring the fish up to us
and we will hold the canoe against the wind.'
So Kurramon dived into the sea
and swam down to the reef where the fish were.
But the clam closed on his hands
and the sea moved into him
and he died under the water.
His brothers, looking down into the sea,
saw that he was dead and they returned with the canoe.

'Now Lamari can choose between us,' said Nabijura.
'I will go to her first for I am the oldest.
If she will not be my wife then you can go and ask her.'
When they had drawn the canoe up on the beach
Nabijura went through the bush to where Lamari lived,
but the little bird had reached there before him
and she was dead
with the spear she had thrust into her side
reaching away from her on the ground.

94

When Nabijura saw this he was afraid.
He ran back to Walara and told him what he had seen.
'Let us go out to the reef again,' he said.
'We will dive down
and free Kurramon's hands from the clam,
then we will bring him alive again
and take him back to his wife.
When he pulls the spear from her side
she will live again and will not be lost to us.'

Then Nabijura and Walara
took their canoe from the beach
and paddled out to the reef
where Kurramon had died.
They looked down into the water
and saw his body moving as the sea moved.
Then it was gone
and a fish of all colours shot up from the reef.
It broke through the surface
and travelled in a curve through the sky
with the speed of a spear.
Behind it the trail of its colour left a rainbow there.
Then Nabijura and Walara went back to the beach
and the rainbow moved with them
till it passed over the bush
and touched the mia-mia where Lamari was lying.
When the colour covered her
she turned into a bread-fruit flower
and grew there under the rainbow.

Now,
when the rain and the sun
visit the world together,
the bread-fruit flower blooms
and the rainbow stands above it.
This will be so for ever.

The starfish

There was once a tribe that lived by the sea,
and their totem was the Starfish.

There was an island
lying off the coast of their country
and the Starfish men longed to visit this island,
for they had heard it was rich in game.
But they had no canoe.

Now, in all this land
the only man who had a canoe
was a member of the Whale tribe
and he was a selfish man
who would never lend his canoe,
nor even allow anyone to share it with him.

A Starfish man
thought about the Whale man and his canoe
and he told his people:
'I will get this canoe for our use,
and we will go to the island.
I have a plan.'
And he became friendly with the Whale man.
When the Whale man needed help
the Starfish man was there to help him.
When a kangaroo fell to the spear of the Starfish man
he gave half to the Whale man.
The Whale man valued his friendship
since it was profitable to him.

One day
the Whale man asked the Starfish man
to come with him in his canoe to catch a turtle.

97

The Starfish man was glad
and he went with him
and they caught a turtle
and brought it back to the beach.

The Starfish man pulled the canoe up on to the sand.
He carried the turtle over the sand-hill
that divided the shore from the bushland,
and here he lit a large fire
and began to cook the turtle.

The canoe could not be seen from the fire,
for this was the Starfish man's intention.
The Whale man sat beside the fire
and watched the Starfish man do all the work,
and the friendship between them
seemed to him a desirable thing.

When the turtle was cooked
the Starfish man said,
'I will get some shells from the beach
so that we can drink the juice of the turtle.
You wait till I return.'
Then he walked over the sand-hill
and waved his hand
and some men of his tribe saw him wave his hand
and they came out on to the beach
for he had instructed them to lie hidden
till he had signalled to them

When he returned to the Whale man
with some shells
the two men began eating the turtle,
and as they ate,
the Starfish man talked.
He told stories that made the Whale man laugh.
He spoke his stories in a loud voice
and he acted the things he told.

While he was doing this,
the Starfish men
who had remained hidden,
took the canoe and paddled away towards the island.

After a while
the Whale man became very still
and he stopped eating and listening
and looked with suspicion at the Starfish man,
for the Starfish man had revealed that he was acting.
Then the Whale man jumped to his feet
and ran to the beach,
and when he saw his canoe out on the sea
he rushed into the water and swam after it.
But the Starfish men paddled strongly
and they drew further away from him.

When the Whale man saw
that he could never catch them
he threw up his arms
and his arms waved in the air.
Then he sank
and became a starfish that waves its arms in the sea.

The origin
of the bull-roarer

In the Dreamtime
the mountains were so high
that the moon was small when it rose above them.
Some of the mountains
were gold and red when the sun was upon them,
and some were always dark and forbidding.

In the dark mountains there lived an evil people,
but in the golden mountains the people were good.
Two brothers had their camp in the golden mountains.
They were each named Byama
and they were both married.
Each had a child
and both children were called Weerooimbrall.
One day the brothers and their wives
left the camp to hunt for food
and the two children were alone.
The children played in the creek and were happy.

One of the evil men
from the dark mountains
was named Thoorkook,
and he kept a number of savage dogs
with which he hunted the men he hated
and the animals he needed for food.
He watched the brothers and their wives
leave the camp,
and when they had gone he called his dogs
and brought them down the mountain,
and when he reached the camp
where the children were playing
he cried out to the dogs
and they fell upon the children and killed them.

101

Then Thoorkook
fled back to his mountain
where he thought he was safe.

When the brothers and their wives returned
and saw what had happened
they were distraught.
The brothers vowed vengeance,
and next morning
they turned themselves into kangaroos
and followed the tracks
of Thoorkook and his dogs ·
into the dark mountains.

When they came to Thoorkook's camp
they moved around it
so that the wind touched them
before it passed over the camp.
When the dogs got the scent of the kangaroos
they began to bay,
and Thoorkook sprang to his feet
and grasped his spears
and his woomera leaning against a tree.
He called to his dogs
and urged them up-wind
where he thought the kangaroos would be found.

The dogs ran in a pack up the hill
and Thoorkook followed,
leaping from rock to rock
and shouting encouragement.

When the two brothers were sighted by the dogs
they raced away with the dogs behind them.
They led the pack down the mountainside
and across a valley
to where a tall cliff
rose like a wall above the trees.

When they reached a clearing
at the foot of the cliff
they made a stand
with their backs to the cliff face.
There they waited.

The leading dogs
burst through the scrub
surrounding the clearing
and hurled themselves at the kangaroos.
But the two brothers were great fighters
and they awaited the dogs without fear.
As the dogs leaped at their throats
the brothers raised their powerful back legs
and slashèd the dogs with their claws
so that the dogs fell back bleeding.
Soon all the dogs were attacking them,
but they fought them off
until all the dogs were dead
or dying on the grass.

Then the brothers followed their tracks
back into the bush
until they met Thoorkook
who was running strongly
so that he might be in at the kill.
And the brothers fell on him and slew him,
and he died on the ground
with his spears in his hand.
Then the brothers changed to men again
and returned to the camp.

Next day they went out hunting
and one of the brothers,
seeing the scratches left by a possum
on the bark of a tree,
took his stone axe and cut notches in the trunk
so that he might climb the tree.

103

When he was high up the trunk
a chip flew from his axe
and went humming through the air
with a sound like the voice of a child.
He climbed quickly down from the tree at the sound,
for it seemed to him
that it was the voice of his child
speaking to him from its Dreaming.
And his brother, too,
heard the voice,
and they picked up the chip and looked at it in wonder.
They decided to keep it
so that they would always remember their little ones.

The brother who had climbed the tree
bored a hole in the end of the chip
and threaded a vine rope through the hole
so that he might carry it
hanging from his shoulder.
But first he swung it round his head
and the voice came again
and it was the voice of their children.
Then the brothers took the chip
and they went from tribe to tribe
and told them of this wonder,
and thereafter men used it
to call the tribes together.
It became the bull-roarer.
And painted men
walked through the bush
and swung their bull-roarers
when ceremonial dances were to be held.
Men of other tribes rallied when they heard it,
for the sound
was a spirit voice from the Dreaming
and its summons must be obeyed.